STAGECOACH
SANTA

STAGECOACH SANTA

Randall A. Reinstedt

Illustrated by Judith L. Macdonald

Ghost Town Publications
Carmel, California

The History and Happenings of California Series
Published by
Ghost Town Publications
P.O. Drawer 5998
Carmel, California 93921

Manufactured in the United States of America

Second Printing

Library of Congress Catalog Number 86-81735
ISBN 0-933818-20-3

Edited by John Bergez
Book Design by Katherine Minerva

This book is dedicated to Carl Edward Browne
and to all who believe in Santa Claus

STAGECOACH SANTA

It was December 24, 1881, and eight-year-old Carl Edward Browne was confused. Tomorrow would be his first Christmas in California, and it wasn't anything like what he was used to.

Back home, in far-off Ohio, Christmas was a time of bare trees and slick frozen ponds you could skate on and plenty of snow. Everything was different now that his family had moved to California. In the little valley where they had settled, the trees were green, the days were warm, and there wasn't a sign of snow or ice anywhere.

The afternoon sun shone brightly as Carl Edward trudged along the old stagecoach road that went by the Brownes' new ranch. It didn't feel a bit like Christmas, and he felt sad and worried.

For one thing, it was hard to be so far away from his best friend, Erick. Out here he had nobody his own age to play with. His one friend was old Charlie Moran, who drove the stagecoach between the valley towns of Soledad and Jolon. Charlie was full of stories about old California. He could sit for

hours on the long, rambling porch of the Jolon Inn, spinning colorful tales of Spanish padres, California Indians, daring bandits, and hardy gold seekers. Sometimes he sent chills running through Carl Edward with his legends of ghosts and lost treasures. Lately he'd even been teaching his young friend how to whittle, and he had promised to show him a thing or two about taking care of horses.

Carl Edward shook his head sadly. Charlie was a good friend, and his company did help to pass the time. Still, it wasn't the same as having a playmate.

But the worst part was Santa Claus. Carl Edward had been worried about Santa Claus ever since the long train ride from Ohio to California. What a huge country it was! He just couldn't understand how Santa would be able to deliver presents to all of the places in Ohio, and all of the other places he had seen on his trip West, and still have time to come to the

Brownes' ranch in California. Why, it had taken the train almost a week just to reach Sacramento!

Carl Edward had loved riding the train, even if he had gotten soot from the smoking engine all over his clothes. All sorts of people had been on board. There were cowboys in their leather vests, well-dressed and funny-talking city folk from New York and Boston, and a few families like his own, headed for a new life in the West. Most of all he had enjoyed seeing the buffalo out on the plains and watching the scenery change as the puffing locomotive hauled the train up over the snowy mountains and down to the broad central valley of the great Golden State. For a while it had all seemed so wonderful and new that he had forgotten his sadness over leaving the farm in Ohio. Then he had realized how very far from home he was and had begun to wonder how Santa Claus would ever manage to find him.

True, his mom and dad said that Santa was used to such trips and would find his way. Still Carl Edward worried. How would Santa know he had moved? Would he know about the fine leather saddle Carl Edward wanted so badly? He had never wished for anything like that before. Besides, whoever heard of Santa Claus and reindeer when there wasn't any snow on the ground? Try as he might, he just couldn't imagine Santa's reindeer pulling a sled full of presents over bumpy paths and rut-filled wagon trails!

"Why did we have to move, anyway?" Carl Edward muttered to himself. He kicked at a stone. "Ohio was swell." He gave the stone another kick and sent it skipping up the trail that led from the stage road to the sagging remains of old Mission San Antonio. The trail made him think of the stories Charlie had told him about the Indians who used to live around the mission in the days of the padres. Did Santa Claus bring them presents, he wondered? Did they even know about the jolly round man and his reindeer? And what about the Chinese that Charlie had told him about, the ones who had found gold in the stream beds nearby? And the miners in the Santa Lucia Mountains, on the other side of the valley? Santa Claus couldn't forget them, could he?

Then again, maybe the gold hunters were too busy to think about Christmas. "Gold makes some people crazy," Charlie had told him one day. "All they can think about is getting rich quick. Your dad's

a wise man to put his muscle and sweat into ranching."

Carl Edward sighed. He was becoming more confused the more he thought! Things had been a lot simpler last Christmas Eve. He remembered building a big snowman in front of the farm house with his friend Erick. At the foot of the snowman they had

left a basket filled with fruit and nuts, hoping that Santa and his reindeer would find the treat.

They had, too! Carl Edward smiled and shivered a little as he remembered running out to the yard early on Christmas morning and finding the basket empty!

But now he was in sunny California. Carl Edward felt a pang of envy as he turned in at the gate of the ranch house. He could just see Erick back home, building a snowman in the yard. There surely wouldn't be any snowman in front of the Brownes' house this year! California might be the "land of plenty," as his dad liked to say. But without snow, and without Santa Claus to bring him a saddle of his own, it sure wasn't the land of plenty for him!

Near the house Carl Edward found his dad busily chopping wood. Sitting down on an old pine stump, he cupped his chin in his hand and watched the axe as it took hungry bites out of a freshly cut log.

"Hello, son!" his father called cheerfully. Carl Edward didn't answer. He couldn't stop thinking about Santa Claus.

Jack Browne gave his axe a rest and took a long look at his son.

"By that frown on your face, young man, I'd say you had a mighty big problem."

Carl Edward nodded and looked away, hoping his father wouldn't see the tears in his eyes. Putting his axe down, Jack Browne walked to the boy's side and put a hand on his shoulder.

"Son, it's time you and I had a talk. Ever since we moved West, you've moped around here feeling sorry for yourself. I know you miss Erick and the other boys, and I know you miss the old farm. But we're in California now, and we're going to have to make the best of it."

"I know, Dad," Carl Edward mumbled, looking at the ground.

"Well, then, how about putting on a happier face for Christmas Eve? I doubt that Santa Claus would be very pleased to see you looking so glum."

Suddenly Carl Edward couldn't keep quiet any longer. He looked tearfully at his father.

"Dad, you keep promising that everything will be fine and that Santa Claus will find his way to our house. But you never tell me how he is going to get here. There's no snow on the ground for his sled. And what if he does come? How is he going to know

where we live? We don't even have our name on the gate!"

"So that's what's bothering you!" his father exclaimed.

Carl Edward sniffled and brushed away a tear. "I've been worried about Santa Claus ever since you told me it doesn't snow in this part of California."

Jack Browne rubbed his chin thoughtfully. "Carl

Edward," he said slowly, "now that we've come West, we have to get used to the way things are done out here."

"You mean Santa isn't coming after all?" Carl Edward cried.

"No, no," his father laughed. "I just mean he has a different way of getting around!"

Carl Edward stared. Now he was really confused!

"Son," his father went on, "you know that stagecoach that comes rumbling past our house most evenings, a little past nine? The one you sometimes hear when you're all snuggled up in bed?"

Carl Edward nodded. "That's Charlie's stage," he said.

"Well, in California, Santa doesn't use a sleigh. Instead, he comes by stagecoach! Tonight, while you're dreaming about that sack full of presents, he'll be speeding here on the Soledad stage!"

"So that's how he does it!" Carl Edward exclaimed. "I wonder why Charlie never told me!"

Jack Browne laughed. "I expect he wanted to keep it a secret. Don't let him know I told you! Now come along and give me a hand with this load of wood. Let's surprise your mother with a big Christmas Eve fire."

"You bet!" cried Carl Edward, and he happily set to work carrying logs into the house.

Everything felt different to Carl Edward now that he knew how Santa Claus would find him. What a wonderful place California was turning out to be! He laughed out loud as he pictured Santa Claus rocking along on a stagecoach and bringing presents to all the homes in the valley. How surprised Erick would be when he wrote and told him how Santa rode the stage that passed the Browne house almost every night!

Just then an idea popped into his head. If Santa was going to be on the evening stage, why couldn't he sneak a look at him as he went by? Then he would really have something to tell Erick!

Of course, he knew that children weren't supposed to wait up for Santa Claus or see him delivering their presents. And he certainly didn't want Santa to be angry with him and not leave that saddle! But what if he went outside, down to his favorite hiding place overlooking the stage road? What harm could there be in taking a quick look as Santa's stage went charging by?

The more he thought about his idea, the better it sounded. Soon his mind was made up. He was going to watch for Santa Claus!

After supper that night, Carl Edward gave a huge yawn.

"I think I'd like to go to bed early tonight," he told his parents. "That way Santa can come sooner, and he'll have more time to bring presents to the other people in the valley."

His mother looked at him with surprise.

"Why, that's fine, dear. It's nice of you to be thinking of others."

"I'm sure Santa will appreciate it," Jack Browne added, with a wink at his wife.

Trying his best to look sleepy, Carl Edward kissed his parents good night. Alone in his room, he shut the door and knelt by the bed to say his evening prayers.

"Bless Mom, bless Dad, bless Erick and Charlie," he whispered. "And please bless Santa so that he has a safe trip tonight!"

Then he slipped under the covers, leaving his clothes on so that he would be ready for the night's adventure. Knowing that his mother would look in

on him later, he pulled the blankets high around his head.

It seemed like hours before he heard the bedroom door softly open.

"Are you asleep, dear?" his mother's voice whispered. Carl Edward lay perfectly still. "Good night, then," his mother said. "Sleep tight." The door shut with a quiet click.

Under the covers, Carl Edward forced himself to wait until he had counted to a hundred. Then he threw off the blankets and crept quietly out of bed. In the moonlight he could see just well enough to unfasten the window. Crawling through the opening, he let himself down to the ground and tiptoed to the front gate. No sound came from the house. With a little shiver of excitement, he opened the gate and started down the stage road.

Overhead the moon was full and bright. With the help of its light, Carl Edward soon reached his hiding place. It was at a bend in the road, where a clump of aged oak trees and twisted manzanita bushes grew among a huge outcropping of rocks.

This was Carl Edward's own special spot. He liked to play around these rocks on sunny afternoons, acting out stories of bandits and heroes he had heard from Charlie Moran. The rocks were full of wonderful hiding places. The best of the bunch was where two gigantic boulders rested against each other and formed a long, narrow cave.

Carl Edward called this place Vasquez Cave. He had named it after Tiburcio Vasquez, a famous California badman whose gang used to visit the valley. According to Charlie, Vasquez was known as the "gentleman bandit," because he sometimes apologized to the people he was robbing! Vasquez Cave looked like just the sort of place where outlaws might hide, and Carl Edward often went looking for signs of bandit treasure that might be buried nearby.

Picking his way through the rocks and trees, Carl Edward came to the entrance of Vasquez Cave. It surely looked different at night! It was so dark inside, he didn't dare go in. Instead he searched about until he found a good lookout between a big rock and an old oak tree. From there he could peek around the rock and see the bend in the stage road.

"I'm just like Vasquez!" he thought. He imagined the bandit lurking silently behind the rock with a gun in his hand, listening for the rumble of the southbound stage approaching the bend. The difference was, Carl Edward wasn't about to jump out and order the stage to stop! All he wanted to do was to stay out of sight and steal a look at Santa Claus going by.

Carl Edward listened hard, but all he could hear was the chirping of crickets and the eerie sound of the wind as it rustled through the trees. Nothing moved on the stage road. After a while, he settled down to wait and began looking around him.

It was then that he began to wonder whether his idea was such a good one after all.

Carl Edward knew the area around Vasquez Cave very well—by day. Now it seemed like a very different place. In the pale light of the moon, the rocks loomed darkly above his head. The limbs of the bent oak trees reached out as if to snatch at him. Behind him the mouth of the cave was huge and black as ink. Carl Edward shuddered. Who knew what might be inside? "Please, Santa," he whispered nervously, "come soon!"

Still the stage road was empty. Clouds from the Pacific began to drift over the Santa Lucia Mountains and played hide and seek with the moon, making strange shadows on the rocks. Remembering Charlie's stories, Carl Edward couldn't help wondering whether the ghosts of Vasquez and his gang were somewhere about, guarding their treasure. Each time the moonlight was blotted out by a cloud, he imagined the spirits of bloodthirsty bandits creeping closer and peering at him from behind the trees.

Carl Edward shivered and tried to keep his teeth from chattering. In his excitement, he had forgotten to take a jacket with him when he left the house. Rubbing his arms up and down, he told himself that it was only the chilly wind that was giving him goosebumps.

It was growing very dark. Carl Edward looked

up and saw that a huge cloud had moved in front of
the moon. It was then that he recalled another of
Charlie's tales—the legend of the Headless Horse-
woman who prowled the hills around Mission San
Antonio. Charlie always laughed when he told ghost
stories, but in the shadowy darkness around Vasquez
Cave they didn't seem funny at all!

Suddenly the moonlight burst through, and

Carl Edward felt his blood run cold. On the top of a nearby hill, a dark shape was standing, motionless. "P-probably just a tree," he stammered to himself. But had it been there before? He couldn't remember. As he stared in fright, a new cloud blocked the moon, plunging the hilltop into darkness. His heart pounded. Enough waiting for Santa Claus! All he could think of now was getting back home.

Hardly daring to move, Carl Edward slowly stood up and started to make his way out of the rocks and trees, away from the shape on the hill.

Then he heard a sound that made him stop in his tracks. It was the blare of a horn—the horn the stagecoach driver blew to let the people at the Jolon Inn know the stage was coming!

Carl Edward froze. If he ran home now, he would miss Santa Claus! Forgetting all about ghosts and headless horsewomen, he scampered back to his hiding place. Crouching behind the rock, he listened for the familiar sounds of the horses' hoofs pounding the hard surface of the stage road. There they were! Closer and closer they came, until he could hear the groaning and creaking of the stagecoach and the crack of the driver's whip. Was Santa Claus really aboard? Cautiously, Carl Edward raised his head and peeked over the rock just as the stage came thundering around the bend.

He could hardly believe his eyes. High atop the coach, one hand gripping the reins and the other snapping a whip, wasn't Charlie, but—a round, jolly

fat man! As the stage rumbled past, Carl Edward could see a white beard blowing in the wind and a red pointed hat that seemed ready to fly from the driver's head with every bounce and jolt of the coach.

Carl Edward rubbed his eyes in disbelief. Were those really antlers he saw on the animals pulling the speeding stage? As he looked again, the whip crackled over their heads and the driver's voice sang out.

"Get a move on, Prancer, you lazy varmint! You, too, Donner! Keep a-pullin' your share of the load, Blitzen! We've many a mile to cover before the sun comes over those mountains yonder!"

It was Santa Claus! Carl Edward couldn't contain himself any longer. Shouting with excitement, he scrambled down to the road and ran after the swaying coach as it neared the entrance to the Browne ranch.

But something was wrong. Instead of slowing down, the stage was picking up speed! Carl Edward stared as the stagecoach sped past the gate to the ranch. "Wait!" he shouted, running all the harder. "Wait!"

It was no use. In a flash the stage was around the far bend and out of sight. The drumming of the hoofbeats grew fainter and fainter until at last they died away. All that remained was a cloud of dust in the air.

Carl Edward stopped running and stood in the middle of the stage road, panting for breath. Surely there was some kind of mistake. Any minute now,

the stage would turn around and he would see it coming back to the ranch. He kept his eyes on the far turn and listened for the sound of hoofbeats approaching.

Nothing happened. Except for the shrill whistle of the wind, the night was silent. Even the crickets had stopped their chirping.

With a terrible, empty feeling growing inside

him, Carl Edward waited and watched until his body ached with the cold. Then he slumped down by the side of the road and began to cry. He had never felt so miserable. How could Santa Claus pass him by? He could hardly bear to think that somehow Santa had forgotten all about him. Or was he so angry that he had decided not to stop? "Please, Santa," he prayed, "you can keep the saddle if you'll just come back!" Time and again he wiped his eyes and looked hopefully at the far turn. There was no sign of the stagecoach. At last, when the tears would no longer come, he climbed to his feet and began to walk slowly back to the ranch house.

The next thing Carl Edward knew, he was being shaken awake.

"Come on, sleepy head, it's Christmas!"

Carl Edward blinked and opened his eyes to find that he was snugly in bed. The bright California sunshine was pouring through his window. His parents smiled down at him.

"Well, don't you want to see what Santa has left for you?" his mother asked.

"But that's impossible!" blurted Carl Edward. "Santa Claus didn't even stop at our house last night!"

"What are you talking about, son?" questioned his father. "Come on out to the fireplace and have a look." Playfully, Jack Browne picked his son up and carried him to the main room.

Carl Edward gasped in surprise. Hanging over the fireplace was a huge stocking bulging with candy and fruit, and beneath the Christmas tree was a pile of gay packages wrapped in bright red and white paper.

"Most of those are for you, I think," his father
said, letting him down.

Overjoyed, Carl Edward ran to the Christmas
tree. Eagerly he lifted one package after another,
searching for the one special present he hoped would
be there. When he reached the bottom of the pile, his
heart fell. None of the gifts was large enough to be
the one he was looking for.

"Well, aren't you going to open at least one?" his father teased. "Santa came an awfully long way just to bring those to you."

Carl Edward bit his lip, trying to hide his disappointment. He knew he couldn't keep his secret any longer. Besides, he badly wanted someone to explain how the presents had got there. Hoping he wouldn't be scolded too badly, he took a deep breath and told his parents about what had happened the night before.

When he had finished his story, his mother looked questioningly at Jack Browne. Then she began to laugh. "Carl Edward," she said, "that was quite a dream you had last night! Imagine Santa Claus driving a stagecoach!"

"But Dad said that Santa uses a stagecoach in California!" Carl Edward exclaimed. "Because there's no snow."

"He's right, Becky, I did say that," agreed Jack Browne from the doorway of his son's room. "And I don't know what Carl Edward saw last night, but the part about sneaking out of the house was no dream. Come over here and have a look."

Carl Edward and his mom followed Jack Browne into the bedroom. Looking in the direction he pointed, they saw a messy pile of clothes on the floor and a window that was still partly open. Jack Browne looked sternly at his son.

"Carl Edward, I don't want to scold you on Christmas, and I know it was what I said that prompted you to sneak out last night. But I think you know better than to go wandering around alone in the dark."

"And the cold," frowned Becky Browne.

Carl Edward hung his head. "I know. I just wanted to tell Erick how wonderful California is and how I saw Santa on his stagecoach."

"What's all this about a stagecoach?" asked his mother. "Where I come from, Santa Claus drives a sleigh."

Jack Browne held up a hand. "I guess this is mostly my fault," he said. "Son, maybe I'd better explain something—"

Before he could finish, they heard the stomp of feet on the front porch and a friendly voice calling out.

"Merry Christmas, folks! That is, if there's anyone awake yet in this lazy household!"

"It's Charlie!" Carl Edward cried. Running to the door, he threw it open. There stood Charlie Moran, dressed in his Sunday-best black suit. In his hands was a carved wooden stagecoach, complete with a team of horses in full gallop. With a smile he handed it to Carl Edward. "Here you are, partner," he said, "hand-made and one of a kind. Be careful of the horses' legs, now. They won't kick, but they might just break."

Carl Edward's eyes grew wide as he took the present from Charlie's outstretched hands. The carving was wonderfully detailed, right down to the horses' flowing manes and the spoked wheels of the

coach. "Wow!" he stammered. "This is beautiful. Thank you, Charlie!" Carefully he stood the carving on a table and stepped back to admire it. "It's beautiful," he repeated. "I'm going to keep it forever!"

Charlie laughed. "Forever is a long time, son. By the way, that's a mighty fine saddle you've got out there. Did Santa Claus bring you that?"

"Saddle!" yelped Carl Edward.

"Saddle?" questioned his father.

"Saddle?" echoed his mother.

"On the fence by the front gate," Charlie replied, nodding toward the door. "You can't hardly miss it. It's the one with the big red bow on it."

Carl Edward was already through the door and racing toward the gate. His parents and Charlie hurried out to join him.

It was just as Charlie had said. Draped across the fence was a boy-sized saddle, wrapped in a bright red bow!

Carl Edward's eyes shone as he ran his hands over the smooth brown leather. Santa Claus hadn't forgotten him after all!

"I told you I saw Santa," he said to his parents. "I bet he just wanted to teach me a lesson. He must have stopped on his way out of the valley instead of on his way in. Boy, wait until I tell Erick about this!"

Jack Browne looked wonderingly at his wife. Then his face broke into a wide smile. "Well, well. I guess you're right, and I hope you did learn something after all. Now why don't you run inside and put on some riding clothes? I'll bet Charlie here wouldn't mind giving you your first lesson in saddling up that pony out back."

Charlie Moran looked down at his Sunday-best suit. "Wouldn't mind a bit," he said with a grin.

"Yippee!" yelled Carl Edward, running toward the house. "Don't anybody move! I'll be right back!" At the door he stopped and called back to his father.

"Dad, you were right all along. California is swell, and this is the best Christmas yet!" With that he disappeared into the house.

Jack Browne smiled and held out his hand to Charlie Moran.

"You really didn't have to do that, Charlie," he said, shaking the older man's hand. "But I sure do appreciate it. I hardly know how to thank you."

Charlie looked at him strangely. "Jack, just what are you talking about?"

"Why, the saddle, of course," answered Jack Browne. "And that was some trick you played last night, dressing up like Santa Claus."

"Carl Edward even thought he saw antlers on your horses," added Becky Browne. Chuckling, they told Charlie all about Carl Edward's adventure of the night before.

The old driver listened to their tale without saying a word. When they had finished, he shook his head.

"I thank you for the thought, folks," he said. "But I don't know anything about any saddle, and that's the truth. It was sitting prettily on the fence when I got here this morning. And as for your stagecoach Santa ..." Charlie was silent for a moment. Then he continued, "You know, that makes three people who say they saw Santa Claus driving my stage last night. The funny thing is, I was home in bed. I'm not due for a run until tomorrow."

Jack and Becky Browne stared in bewilderment. "Then ... who?" asked Becky.

Charlie Moran shrugged and gazed thoughtfully down the old stage road.

"I only know one thing," he said quietly. "And that is—there ain't been a stagecoach out of Soledad for three days!"

AUTHOR'S NOTES

Stagecoach Santa is based on a tale that has long been known to people of California's history-rich Monterey County. I first learned of the story in 1969, when a much shorter version of it appeared in the *Monterey Peninsula Herald* newspaper. This anonymous version apparently was found in a scrapbook kept by a long-time resident of the area and subsequently given to the Monterey History and Art Association.

Intrigued by the brief newspaper account, I filed it away, hoping to find time one day to expand the story and retell it to the young people of today. It is my belief that stories of this kind add a touch of romance to our colorful past, and to our ever-expanding collection of California lore.

A number of years went by, during which I taught school at the fourth-grade level and wrote several children's stories and many history-oriented magazine articles and books. It wasn't until 1986 that I dipped into my file and decided to begin the enjoyable task of writing a new version of the remarkable tale of Monterey County's "Stagecoach Santa." Unfortunately, while I still had the *Herald's* account, efforts to locate the scrapbook in which the story had been found proved unsuccessful.

Only after the first printing of this book appeared did I learn that all of us who are charmed by the legend of Stagecoach Santa are indebted to Hal McClure, a writer for the *King City Rustler* whose byline appears above a short version of the tale, published in the *Rustler* on December 22, 1949.

Evidently it was this story that made its way into some history-lover's scrapbook and, twenty years later, into the newspaper article that eventually inspired my adaptation.

Although the basic theme of the story remains the same in my retelling (along with the location and the main characters), the tale has been modified and greatly expanded for dramatic interest and historical perspective. My hope is that stories involving real historical settings can make the past come alive for young readers, so that they will want to learn more about our history and heritage. With this in mind, let me present some factual information about the people, places, and events mentioned in the text.

Monterey County was one of California's original twenty-seven counties. Located along the Pacific Coast section of central California, it is bordered by the counties of Santa Cruz, San Benito, Fresno, Kings, and San Luis Obispo. Monterey County is noted for its natural beauty, especially along its scenic shoreline. Its imposing **Santa Lucia Mountains** border the Pacific Ocean and add to the grandeur of the rugged coast. Inland lie fertile valleys, notably the Salinas Valley, which has been described as one of the most productive agricultural valleys in the world. Among the county's historic communities, Monterey is the best known. Founded in 1770, Monterey served as the capital of California under both Spanish and Mexican rule.

Monterey County played an important part in California's colorful Mission Period. **Mission San Antonio** (San Antonio de Padua) was the third church in Father Junipero Serra's chain of California missions. Established in 1771, it became one of the most interesting and beautiful of the early missions. In 1805 its population reached a high of nearly 1,300 **California Indians.**

Both the mission and the nearby community of **Jolon** are located in the beautiful San Antonio Valley. Each has survived to this day and can be visited by those who are interested. (After falling into decay, Mission San Antonio's church was restored in the 1940s.) A little over thirty miles to the north, in the Salinas Valley, is the community of **Soledad.**

The **miners** in the Santa Lucia Mountains and the **Chinese gold seekers** that are mentioned in the text played a part in the early history of south Monterey County. Many of the Chinese are said to have found their way to the area from California's famed gold country in the Sierra Nevada and from a large Chinese fishing village that once thrived on the shores of Monterey Bay.

The Chinese gold hunters are reported to have found gold in the area near Jolon and Mission San Antonio. Their success prompted prospectors from other places to come to the Santa Lucias and try their luck in the coastal peaks.

Considerable gold was found over a period of many years, and in 1875 the Los Burros Mining District was formed. A mining town known as Manchester also sprang up in the coastal mountains. (The name of the town was later changed to Mansfield.) This small mining community was lost to fire around the turn of the century and today is referred to as "the lost city of the Santa Lucias."

The **Jolon Inn** was a real stage stop and popular gathering place in the early days. Old-timers also knew it as the Dutton Hotel. Unfortunately, little is left of this aged adobe structure, but a marker located along Monterey County road G14 reminds travelers of the colorful part it played in local history.

Those who seek the site of the Jolon Inn may also wish to obtain a detailed map of the area and locate Oro Fino (Fine Gold) Canyon and two additional sites, each known as China Gulch. These locations are described as having yielded gold to early Chinese placer miners. Perhaps at this point a word of caution is in order: visitors and future gold seekers should be aware that today much of the area is government owned and is part of the Hunter Liggett Military Reservation. Permission must be obtained for off-road exploration of both private and public land.

The subject of gold brings to mind bandits and bandit treasure. As described in the text, one of the most famous of California's early badmen was **Tiburcio Vasquez.** Born in Monterey in 1835, Vasquez began his notorious career of crime when he was a teenager. He was convicted of murder and hung in San Jose, California, in 1875. During his bandit career he was described as a stagecoach robber, cattle thief, Robin Hood, and killer, all rolled into one. He was also a talented horseman and the leader of his own outlaw gang.

Vasquez and his followers, as well as other California badmen, were known to have frequented south Monterey County. Tales of lost **bandit treasures** are discussed to this day by old-timers of the area.

Among numerous other stories told by both long-time residents and newcomers to the Jolon–Mission San Antonio area are tales of a mysterious **headless horseback rider.** The headless rider is often described as being a woman of Indian descent, and stories of her ghostly appearances are said to date back more than 100 years.

Legends, tales, mysteries: California history is filled with them! Along with well-documented facts, they are all part of our colorful past. Now that you know the behind-the-scenes story of *Stagecoach Santa*, I hope you'll want to continue exploring the fascinating heritage of the Golden State.

ABOUT THE AUTHOR

Randall A. Reinstedt was born and raised on California's beautiful and historic Monterey Peninsula. After traveling widely throughout the world, he spent fifteen years teaching elementary school students, with special emphasis on California and local history. Today he continues to share his love of California's beauty and lore with young and old alike through his immensely popular publications. Among his many books is *More than Memories: History and Happenings of the Monterey Peninsula,* an acclaimed history text for fourth-graders that is used in schools throughout the Monterey area.

Randy lives with his wife, Debbie, and son, Erick, in a house overlooking the Pacific Ocean. In addition to his writing projects, he is in great demand as a lecturer to school and adult groups, and he frequently gives workshops for teachers on making history come alive in the classroom.

ABOUT THE ARTIST

Judith Laurel Macdonald was born in Sydney, Australia. Although she has attended the National Art School of Sydney as well as many workshops and classes, she considers herself a self-taught artist, working mainly in watercolor and ink. Among her credits are the illustrations for several elementary-school textbooks.

Before creating the art for *Stagecoach Santa,* Judith explored the Jolon area, recording on sketch pad, film, and memory the ruins of the Jolon Inn, Mission San Antonio, and the surrounding landscape.

Randall A. Reinstedt's
History and Happenings of California Series

Through colorful tales drawn from the rich store of California lore, this series introduces young readers to the historical heritage of California and the West. "Author's Notes" at the end of each volume provide information about the people, places, and events encountered in the text. Whether read for enjoyment or for learning, the books in this series bring the drama and adventure of yesterday to the young people of today.

Currently available:
Stagecoach Santa
ISBN 0-933818-20-3
Otters, Octopuses, and Odd Creatures of the Deep
ISBN 0-933818-21-1

California history and lore are also featured in Randy Reinstedt's books for adults and older children. For information about these titles, please write Ghost Town Publications, P.O. Drawer 5998, Carmel, California 93921.